Safe Surfing on the Internet

THE INTERNET LIBRARY

Safe Surfing
on the Internet

Art Wolinsky

Enslow Publishers, Inc.

40 Industrial Road	PO Box 38
Box 398	Aldershot
Berkeley Heights, NJ 07922	Hants GU12 6BP
USA	UK

http://www.enslow.com

Library of Congress Cataloging-in-Publication Data

Wolinsky, Art.
      Safe surfing on the Internet / Art Wolinsky.
         p. cm. — (The Internet library)
      Summary: Explores the many safety issues involved in using the
Internet, including the relevant laws, especially CIPA and COPPA,
acceptable use policies (AUPs), and other protection and privacy issues.
      Includes bibliographical references and index.
      ISBN 0-7660-2030-4
      1. Internet and children—United States—Juvenile literature. 2.
Computer crimes—United States—Prevention—Juvenile literature. 3.
Internet—Safety measures—Juvenile literature. [1. Computer
crimes—Prevention. 2. Internet—Safety measures. 3. Safety.] I. Title.
II. Series.
HQ784.I58 W65 2003
004.67'8—dc21

                            2002012336

Printed in the United States of America

10 9 8 7 6 5 4 3 2 1

Contents

Introduction

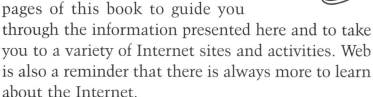

This is my friend Web. He will appear throughout the pages of this book to guide you through the information presented here and to take you to a variety of Internet sites and activities. Web is also a reminder that there is always more to learn about the Internet.

Web takes his work seriously, even the occasional bad pun. (It takes creativity and hard thinking to make a really good, bad pun.) Lately though, Web has been a little upset. He has been complaining that his job has been getting harder and harder, because there are a lot of new laws, rules, and regulations he has to follow. He is also getting a lot of junk mail and some not-so-nice people are contacting him. All of these things combine to make his Internet surfing more difficult than it has been in the past.

The government is passing laws about computer use and the Internet. Many schools also require students and parents to read and sign computer-use contracts or Acceptable Use Policies. There are specific ways to deal with people online, Internet safety, and privacy.

Web is upset that many of these things are happening, but he understands why they are necessary. We felt it would be a good idea to write a book that would give you some advice and explain the new laws and rules that effect you and your use of the Internet. We don't want to just tell you the rules. We want you to understand the reasons behind them and why they are important. That way you won't be upset when you come in contact with them.

I can guess what you are thinking. You are probably thinking, "Right! I'm really going to take advice from a guy who talks to cartoon characters." If that is what you are saying to yourself, I should also tell you that I often talk to myself, but that's okay. A wise person once told me that it was okay if I talked to myself. It was also okay if I argued with myself, but that if I lost the arguments, I was in big trouble. So far I have not lost any arguments with myself.

So, now that you know where Web's bad puns come from, we can get on with the book.

Chapter 1

When Did You Learn Your First Rule?

You can't get away from rules. Rules are all around us. There are rules of nature, rules of language, and rules of math. There are school rules, religious rules, and laws made by our government. Rules tell us what is right or wrong, good or bad, safe or unsafe. Rules shape our world.

Did you ever stop to think about how many rules there are, how we learn them, or why we have to follow them? When was the first time you came in contact with rules? How old were you? What was the rule? Think about it for a minute. I will wait. . . .

OK, now that you've thought about it, how old were you? Did you say three years old? Did you say four years old? Did you say you were older than that? Did you say you were younger? Did you say you were a few months old? If you said you were a baby, you were right.

When you were a baby, you cried when you were hungry and you cried when you were uncomfortable. You didn't think about it. You just did it. As time passed, you learned that if you were hungry and cried, you would get fed. You learned that if your diapers were wet and you cried, you got changed.

As time passed, your parents could tell a hungry cry from a wet-diaper cry, or an angry cry from

Learning Rules:

If you think babies can't learn rules, you can read about some experiments that showed babies can understand language-like math rules. You can even do the experiment at <http://abcnews.go.com/sections/science/DailyNews/babylanguage981231.html> or <http://www.psych.nyu.edu/gary/babylab.html>.

a hurt cry. Of course, you had your laugh, your smile, and your babble to add to your pre-language communication.

Sometime early in your life, your parents felt it was time for you to start learning things. One of the first things you learned was that meals are not always served on demand. At some time, your parents decided it was time for you to get on a regular feeding schedule. You suddenly came into contact with your first rule.

On Your Screen

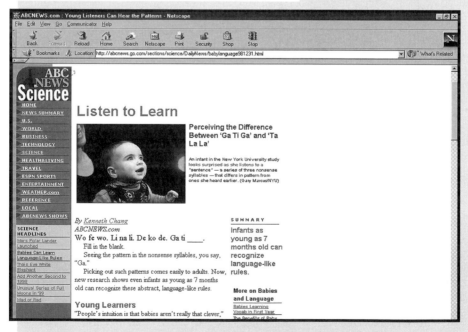

Experiments have shown that even babies can understand and learn language-like rules.

▶ Learning Rules Can Be Tough

You got hungry and started your hungry cry. Your mother decided it was too early to feed you. Your hungry cry did not work. You may have moved on to an angry cry. Eventually, when your parents decided it was time, you got fed and, eventually, you learned that there were feeding times.

Rules, Rules, Rules!
Sometimes there seem to be so many rules to remember.

Rules of Life:

You may have learned to follow some rules by getting punished. For instance, many children learn that you don't write on walls with crayons. Sometimes punishment is not enough. Sometimes we learn the hard way. You may have learned some rules by getting hurt. For instance, you may have reached for the stove and your mother may have yelled, "No! Don't touch! Hot!" She may even have smacked your hand.

For some of you that might not have been enough. So you waited until your mom was out of sight before you touched it. That might have been very painful, but you understood that there was a reason for the rule. When you understand the reason for rules, it is much easier to follow them.

▶ Rules, Schools, and Ruling the World

Just when you were learning the rules of the house, it was time for you to learn a new set of rules. You had to go to school.

Why do you go to school? That may sound like a silly question, but think about it for a minute. I will wait, again. . . .

OK, what was your answer? Did you say something like, "I go to school to learn to read, do math, science, and other stuff?"

If you did, you would be partly right. Sure reading, math, and science are things you have to learn, but they are not the only reason you go to school. You go to school to learn about life and what it takes to run the world.

Reading + Writing + Mathematics + History + Science + Teamwork + Problem Solving = LIFE

You may not have thought about running the world, but look around you. In your class are the future doctors, lawyers, politicians, authors, and every occupation that will make up your world when you grow up.

You need reading, science, and math skills to do many jobs, but you also need to know about citizenship and teamwork. You must learn about problem solving, personal privacy, safety, and other things that make you a good citizen. You will not find any courses called Citizenship 101 or Advanced Safety, because these are things you should be practicing twenty-four hours a day, everywhere you go. They are part of the rules of life.

▶ Rules for the Times

Rules change over time. Things that were not important in past years may become important today. For example, there are traffic rules that say you should stay a safe distance behind the car in front of you. That is an important rule, but it was not important before cars. Did you ever hear of a fifty-horse pileup on the Oregon Trail?

In the early 1900s, there was a transportation revolution. Trains where changing the way we traveled in groups. They replaced horse-drawn coaches. Cars began to take over for horses.

People were used to horses. They did not understand the power and danger of cars. Cars crashed into cars, and cars crashed into horses. Just take a look at what was happening in Chicago during that period of time. More people died because of car accidents than because of horse accidents. The rules of travel were changing because a new technology (cars) was taking the place of an old technology (horse and wagon).

Archive Photo

In the early 1900s, cars began to replace horses as the primary means of transportation.

Fact Sheet

Year	Horse-Related Deaths	Total Horses	Horse-Related Deaths per 1000	Car-Related Deaths	Total Cars	Car-Related Deaths per 1000
1908	59	53,678	1.1	18	5,475	3.3
1916	79	46,662	1.7	235	65,651	3.6
1930	2	9,550	0.2	843	478,204	1.8

This chart shows how the number of car accidents dropped once people began to understand the new car technology.

As cars took over, the death rate due to car accidents went up until people learned the rules and understood the new technology. By 1930, the number of deaths due to car accidents had dropped dramatically.

Internet Addresses · Communication Facts · How Can I Be Safe?

Here are some real laws that should have been removed a long time ago. They may have made sense long ago, but now they are just plain silly. Some were silly when they were made.

<http://www.dumblaws.com/>

Chapter 2

From Transportation Revolution to Information Revolution

When rules change because the times change, it is often confusing for many people. We are in such a time right now. We are changing the way we communicate and the way we learn. This is actually a much bigger change than the change from horses to cars. That change was something that adults had to worry about. The rules were mostly for them. They drove the cars. The information revolution, the dangers, and the rules are just as important to children as they are to adults, maybe even more important.

Today, the Internet has opened up communications in ways we never imagined. In the 1700s, it took months for a message to get from the East Coast to the West Coast of the United States, because it had to go by ship all the way around South America. With the opening of overland trails, railroads, and the Pony Express, a message could travel from coast to coast in a few weeks. The telegraph sent messages in a matter of minutes. Today, e-mail travels around the world in the blink of an eye and anyone can be in contact with anyone.

This kind of communication is new to everyone. It is a wonderful, powerful tool, but in many ways it is like the car. Many of us do not understand the power and the dangers that come along with this wonderful new tool. You have the ability to help many people, but if you use it carelessly, it can hurt people. What you say and do online can have real impact on people. You can do real damage, or tremendous good.

The world of the Internet did not exist when your parents were children. It is new to them and it may be new to you. The rules are new and we all have to learn them together. Your parents and teachers know how to prepare you to be a good citizen in the face-to-face world, but things are different on the Internet. Things you do are different when people can't see you and you can't see them.

All of the things you are learning about being a good citizen in life have to carry over to the Internet. On the Internet, you have to learn how to be a good netizen. A good netizen has a set of online rules that help guide him or her.

Instant mail:
Today, messages and e-mails can be sent at lightening speed!

▶ Complicated Rules for the Internet

The Internet explosion has resulted in a lot of rules and laws. Some of them are common sense and others seem to make little or no sense. There are three basic kinds of rules you must be aware of—laws, netiquette, and rules set by your school. Regardless of whether or not they seem to make sense, they effect you in some way and it is important to know about them.

Netiquette is a set of unofficial rules of conduct on the Internet. Netiquette is much like Emily Post's rules of etiquette that tell us the way people are supposed to behave in polite, face-to-face society. I talked a lot about netiquette in my book *Communicating on the Internet*, but I will not go into detail here, because a lot of netiquette is contained in the rules your school has built into their Acceptable Use Policy. I will be spending a lot of time talking about that.

▶ COPPA—The Children's Online Privacy and Protection Act

Before I talk about school rules, I want to make you aware of some laws that effect you, your parents, and your school. If you are under thirteen and have

| Internet Addresses | Communication Facts | How Can I Be Safe? |

If you want to find out more about etiquette or netiquette, you can visit some of these Web pages.

Arlene Rinaldi's User Guidelines and Netiquette
<http://www.fau.edu/netiquette/netiquette.html>

Here's a complete online book of Netiquette
<http://www.albion.com/netiquette/book/index.html>

Emily Post's complete book of etiquette
<http://www.bartleby.com/95/>

been using the Web for a while, you may wonder why you were suddenly locked out of some of your favorite sites. When you visited, you may have gotten a message that you needed your parent's permission. This is because of a law that was put into effect in April of 2000.

It is called the Children's Online Privacy and Protection Act (COPPA) and was established partly because advertisers and Web sites were collecting information about children and selling it to businesses that wanted to sell things to children. Many of them were using pretty sneaky methods to gather a lot of information that your parents would not want you to share about yourself or them. COPPA says that if a child can share information on a commercial Web site, even accidentally, it is illegal for that site to allow a child under thirteen to even visit their Web site without written permission from a parent.

A commercial Web site usually ends in a .com and is created by a company that sells things. It is different from school or non-profit Web sites that usually end in .org and are not in the business of selling things. COPPA does not apply to schools and non-profit sites.

You can't get in trouble for visiting a site if they are not following the law. If you are under thirteen, however, you should know that the site is breaking the law if it asks you to share any information without getting written permission from your parents first.

Different types of sites:
It's good to know the difference between .com sites and .org sites.

You and your parents should also know that while you are in school, schools act as your parents and grant permission for you to visit sites. It is important for your parents to know this in case there are certain sites they do not want you to visit, even if the school allows it. In that case, your parents should send a note to the school.

COPPA also says that every commercial Web site must have an easy-to-find, easy-to-understand privacy policy that tells you what they plan on doing with information that is collected. If you see that they are going to share or sell that information with others, it is not a good idea to give out that information.

▶ CIPA—Children's Internet Protection Act

The Children's Internet Protection Act was passed in October of 2000. It is designed to protect you against adult sites that are not appropriate for children. The law says that any school or library that gets money from the government must put Internet filtering software in place. Filtering software automatically blocks users from getting to certain sites on the Internet.

Many people are very angry about CIPA. They do not think the government should be telling people what they can visit and what they cannot. Some think that children should be taught how to handle information properly and filtering is not necessary. Others think that the school or the library, not the government, should make the decision.

About 60 percent of the schools in the United

States had already made the decision to filter before CIPA was passed. Your school may be one of them. If you have ever received any kind of message telling you that your school forbids you to visit the site you were trying to reach, your school is probably filtering.

If you were trying to go to a site that has good content, you probably wondered why it was blocked. This is part of why people are so angry. They say that filters do not work well, and they are right. Filters do protect you from a lot of bad sites, but they

Internet Addresses   Communication Facts   How Can I Be Safe?

There are many sites that will provide you and your parents with information about COPPA, CIPA, and filtering. Here are a few:

COPPA
WiredKids
<http://www.wiredkids.org>

Federal Trade Commission
<http://www.ftc.gov/bcp/conline/edcams/kidzprivacy/kidz.htm>

CIPA
FilteringInfo.org
<http://www.filteringinfo.org/>
This is a site created by one of the filtering software companies.

The American Library Association
<http://www.ala.org/cipa/>
This organization wants to do away with CIPA.

On Your Screen

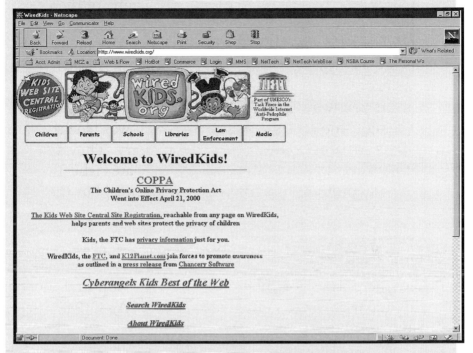

The WiredKids Web site will provide you with useful information about COPPA and other safety and privacy issues that are important to you and your parents.

also block a lot of good sites, and they do let some bad material through. Even Congress recognized that fact when it passed CIPA and cautioned that filters should be just one part of keeping children safe on the Internet.

Some people feel that CIPA violates the United States Constitution that guarantees freedom of speech. They say that because filters block things that people have a right to see, that it is a violation of free speech.

The arguments against CIPA will be presented in the courts and the Supreme Court will probably have the final say. However, even if the Supreme Court rules against CIPA, it will not impact schools because the lawsuit was filed first for public libraries. If that case is settled, a suit for school libraries might be filed. That means CIPA will be around schools for at least a few years until the court cases are settled.

On Your Screen

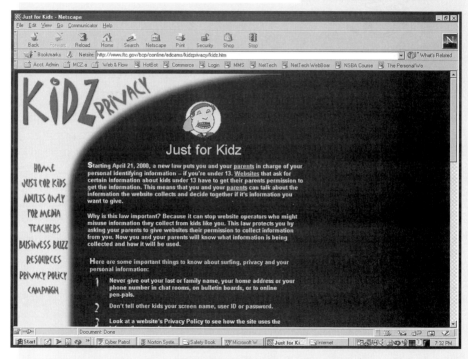

This Web site explains the new Internet safety laws that affect the way you will be able to use and access Internet sites. It also gives tips on how to behave online.

Chapter 3

Acceptable Use Policies and Schools

Today, just about every school that is connected to the Internet has something called an Acceptable Use Policy (AUP). That is pronounced as if you were spelling the letters out one at a time (A-U-P). The AUP is a set of guidelines or rules for using the school's computer network and Internet. You and your parents may have had to sign a copy before the school would let you use the computers and the Internet. The AUP should also include information about your safety, privacy, and the laws that are designed to protect you and your fellow classmates.

In case you are wondering why you need this book if you have laws and an AUP, you probably haven't taken a look at the laws or your school's policy. They are usually written in language that would put you to sleep after the third sentence. If you need proof, here are three sentences from the AUP of the Bellingham School District in Washington State. The Bellingham AUP is one of the best known policies on the Internet and is used as a model by many schools, but you can see that it is aimed at adults.

Telecommunications, electronic information sources and networked services significantly alter the information landscape for schools by opening classrooms to a broader array of resources. In the past, instructional and library media materials could usually be screened—prior to use—by committees of educators and community members intent on subjecting all such materials to reasonable selection criteria. Board Policy 2311 requires that all such materials be consistent with district-adopted guides, supporting and enriching the curriculum while taking into account the varied instructional needs, learning styles, abilities and developmental levels of the students.

Now that was a mouthful! Are you still awake? Even if you did stay awake through those three sentences, you probably do not understand them. Imagine what it is like reading many pages like this. Here is what it means in plain English.

In the past, teachers chose material in the library. With the Internet, there is a lot of junk, bad material, and material that has nothing to do with school. The teachers would never have chosen that material for the library. So when you use the Internet, it should be to get material that deals with things you are doing in school and things that would be chosen for the school library.

▶ Simple Rules for the Internet

Some schools do have AUPs written in language students can understand. This is good, but simply writing the rules isn't good enough. You really need to know the reasons behind the rules.

If your school doesn't already have an AUP, you

Internet Addresses

If you want to see some more examples of AUPs, here are some links to follow.

This is a link to the Bellingham AUP.
<http://www.bham.wednet.edu/2313inet.htm>

Here is a template for the University of Oregon AUP used by some schools.
<http://responsiblenetizen.org/templates/model_policy.html>

Here is a template in simpler English that some schools use.
<http://connectedteacher.classroom.com/tips/aup.asp>

might want to bring it to the attention of your teacher and offer to help write it. I think students should have input into the AUP. After all, it affects them the most. This section can help you and your school develop a policy that everyone understands.

Here is one of the best policies written in plain English. It was created by Parry Aftab, one of the nation's top Internet safety experts. It can be found at the CyberAngels Web site:

<http://www.cyberangels.org/101/index.html>

CyberAngels is an organization devoted to protecting children online. It is a family AUP, but schools are free to change it and use it as they see fit.

▶ My Agreement About Using the Internet

I want to use our computer and the Internet. I know that there are certain rules about what I

On Your Screen

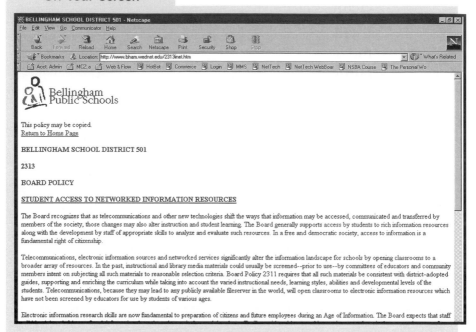

The AUP for the Bellingham Public Schools in Washington
can be used as a model for the AUP at your own school.

should do online. I agree to follow these rules and
my parents agree to help me follow these rules:

1. I will not give my name, address, telephone
   number, school, or my parents' names,
   address, or telephone number, to anyone I
   meet on the computer.

2. I understand that some people online
   pretend to be someone else. Sometimes they
   pretend to be kids, when they're really
   grown-ups. I will tell my parents about
   people I meet online. I will also tell my
   parents before I exchange any e-mail with
   new people I meet online.

3. I will not buy or order anything online

without asking my parents or give out any credit card information.

4. I will not fill out any form online that asks me for any information about myself or my family without asking my parents first.

5. I will not get into arguments or fights online. If someone tries to start an argument or fight with me, I won't answer him or her and will tell my parents.

6. If I see something I do not like or that I know my parents don't want me to see, I will click on the "back" button or log off.

7. If I see people doing things or saying things to other kids online I know they're not supposed to do or say, I'll tell my parents.

8. I won't keep online secrets from my parents.

9. If someone sends me any pictures or any e-mails using bad language, I will tell my parents.

10. If someone asks me to do something I am not supposed to do, I will tell my parents.

11. I will not call anyone I met online, unless my parents say it's okay.

12. I will never meet in person anyone I met online, unless my parents say it's okay.

13. I will never send anything to anyone I met online, unless my parents say it's okay.

14. If anyone I met online sends me anything, I will tell my parents.

Learn the Rules:
It's not so difficult to remember all these rules!

15. I will not use something I found online and pretend it's mine.

16. I won't say bad things about people online, and I will practice good netiquette.

17. I won't use bad language online.

18. I know that my parents want to make sure I'm safe online, and I will listen to them when they ask me not to do something.

19. I will help teach my parents more about computers and the Internet.

20. I will practice safe computing, and check for viruses whenever I borrow a disk from someone or download something from the Internet.

▶ Rules Are Only Part of the Story

Complicated rules and simple rules tell you what you should and should not do, but they do not usually tell you why you should follow them. If you are the type of person who always follows rules, knowing why rules are made may not be that important to you. However, many people are not satisfied with just being told to do something. If you are one of those people, you probably want more information.

You may feel that you are very comfortable with the computer, but an AUP has nothing to do with your skill on the computer. Knowing how to drive a car does not make you a skilled driver or a safe driver, and knowing how to use a computer does not mean you can use it wisely and safely. The AUP is like your driver's manual. It helps you use the computer for learning, communicating, and preparing for life.

An unskilled driver can hurt himself and others. If you do not know the rules of cyberspace, it can cause serious problems for you and others. Or, others can cause serious problems for you. Understanding your AUP can keep you from getting into trouble or getting hurt.

To help you become a good netizen, I will try to explain AUPs and why they are important. I will explain why some things that are okay to do at home with your computer are not okay in school. I hope to take the adult language and legal mumbo-jumbo that you often find in some complicated AUPs and turn it into plain English. I hope to take the simple rules that you already understand and give you the reasons behind them. When you finish reading this book, you will be better prepared take your place as a leader of tomorrow's world. You will be the one making the rules and you want them to be the best they can be.

Understanding your AUP can keep you and others from getting hurt.

▶ Why Do We Need an AUP?

What you do in your home can help or hurt your family members. There are rules you must follow at home. What you do in your class can help or hurt your classmates. There are rules you must follow in school. What you do at your computer when you are on the Internet can help or hurt you, your family, and hundreds or even thousands of people you never met. There are rules you must follow online.

If you do not understand how you can help or hurt thousands of other people, you are not alone. The Internet is a new, powerful tool. A single person can make an impact on the world. That impact can be good or bad. Understanding the AUP is a big step in understanding how both of these things can happen. It can keep you from making mistakes that hurt others. It will guide you to safe, productive use of the computer. Understanding all this can help you make the world a better place.

I will let you in on another secret. The AUP is

| Internet Addresses | Communication Facts | How Can I Be Safe? |

Here are links to student computer activities that had an impact on people in other places.

Students at Southern Regional High School did a project that ended up with TV coverage by five Japanese TV stations.
<http://www.srsd.org/etajima>

Students create Web sites that help thousands learn and earn them $25,000 scholarships.
<http://www.thinkquest.org>

I*EARN has dozens of projects in which students learn from each other and create publications that help many others.
<http://www.iearn.org>

Midlink Magazine **is created by children, for children. It is read by thousands of people. You can submit your work and perhaps have it published.**
<http://www.ncsu.ed/midlink>

On Your Screen

Southern Regional High School students identified the ten people from this fifty-three-year-old photograph and had a teleconference covered by Japanese television.

also there for the benefit of your teachers. Just as the Internet may be a new experience to you, it may be just as new to your teachers. When it comes to the Internet, both you and your teachers may be students.

Finally, the AUP is there for your parents. It tells your parents how the school is using the technology. It tells them what the school is doing to insure your safety online. It tells them what the school expects of you and them when it comes to using computers for learning.

▶ What Is in an AUP?

There are many sections to an AUP. I could print our school's AUP here, but I already told you that it would probably put you to sleep. Besides, it would take up the next fifteen pages. Instead, we will look at some things that are contained in most AUPs.

AUPs deal with safety, privacy, and respecting the property and rights of others. Most start with a section that gives general information about the school's technology network and its use. It will probably tell you that the purpose of the network is to support the teaching and learning that takes place in the school and that other uses are not acceptable. What is and is not acceptable is not always clear.

▶ Acceptable Use and Appropriate Use

If you ask most people what AUP stands for, they will say, Acceptable Use Policy. I would rather use the phrase Appropriate Use Policy. If something is unacceptable, we tend to think that it is bad. Bad things that people do with computers such as hacking, sending threatening messages, or using bad language are just plain wrong and are not acceptable under any conditions. You probably do not have to be reminded not to do those kinds of things.

However, AUPs often tell you that you cannot do things in school that you often do at home, such as visit chat rooms, send jokes, play games, or visit music and sports Web sites. That does not mean schools consider those activities bad. A better word than bad is inappropriate.

Inappropriate is a big word. It simply means something that is not right for the time and place you are doing it. For example, it is appropriate to wear a bathing suit to go to the beach, but it is inappropriate to wear a bathing suit to math class. Some things that are appropriate for you to do at home are not appropriate for you to do in school. A closer look at some of these activities will give an idea of what I mean.

▶ Respecting the Property of Others

The school computers and the school network do not belong to you. They are on loan to you from the school. The AUP tells you how the school expects you to treat the computers and how you should use them.

If I lent you my blue bike and you decided to change the seat height, adjust the handlebars, and paint it red, I would be angry, because it was not your bike. The same thing is true of computers in school. You customize your home computer to look and perform the way you like it. You may change icons, rearrange the desktop, install and remove programs. All of these things are perfectly acceptable on your home computer. In fact, they are the things that help you be more productive or get more enjoyment out of your computer. However, doing these things in school will almost always be a violation of the AUP and will get you in trouble.

We should all learn to respect other people's property.

The computer does not belong to you. Many different people use it. It is not that schools think changing things is wrong or bad. It is because making changes actually costs the school money and interferes with teaching and learning.

In school, five or six people may use each computer during the day. Twenty or thirty different people may use it over the course of a week, and possibly hundreds during the school year. It is very important that the computer looks and acts the same way for everyone. If they do not see the same thing, the teacher may have to stop teaching and fix the problem. That means that every small change can interrupt the education of a whole class of students. If you installed or changed something that conflicts with one of the other programs, the computer may become unusable to many people until it is repaired.

So, you see that small changes you make on your home computer can be a big deal if you make them in school. It can cost money and result in lost learning.

▶ Passwords and Sharing Accounts

Your account and your password are very valuable things. You should never lend them to anyone. Suppose I lent you a book and told you to take good care of it. You promised me you would take good care of it. Then, instead of taking good care of it, you lent it to someone who destroyed it or lost it. Who is to blame and who should pay? It does not matter to me that someone else destroyed it. I lent it to you, and you promised to take good care of it. I expect you to pay for the book.

The same thing is true of your password and your account. The school is giving you a password and an account. When you sign the AUP, you promise not to share the password of the account. If you do share it, and someone does something

Your Computer Screen

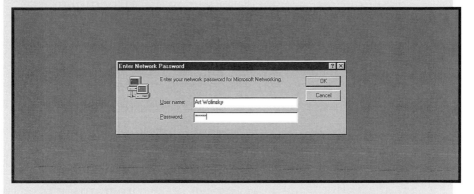

You should always be careful that no one sees you type in your password. This is the best way to protect it from being stolen.

wrong using your password, you may be blamed and lose your computer privileges. Even if you can prove you did not cause the problem, you still broke your promise to not share your password and may have to pay the price for breaking your promise.

You may say, "What if someone steals my password?" The most likely way for someone to steal your password is if you let them see you typing it in. Always hide your password and do not let others watch as you type it in. If you think someone might know your password, change it if your system allows. If your system does not allow you to change your own password, tell your teacher or system administrator that someone knows your password and request a change.

▶ Visiting Inappropriate Sites

Are you beginning to see that what you do on computers can have an impact on others? Are you beginning to see that what is perfectly appropriate on your home computer is not appropriate on your school computer? Let us take a look at another example of how your home computer is different from your school computer.

You do not need an AUP to tell you that visiting adult-only sites or sites that promote dangerous behavior is inappropriate, but you might wonder why visiting a music site, a sports site, or a game site is inappropriate. There are a few good reasons.

The first should be obvious. Unless your teacher has made those sites part of a lesson, you should probably be doing something that deals with class work. If you were in a math class, science class, or any other class and you took out a sports magazine or music magazine, that would be inappropriate. The same is true of visiting those kinds of Web sites when you are supposed to be doing schoolwork.

The second reason is less obvious. Sports, game, and music sites often involve sound, video, and multimedia that present problems for schools. I do not mean that they are annoying or distracting. I am talking about something called bandwidth. Accessing sound or video puts a big strain on any Internet connection. At home, it slows things down for you. In school, the more people using sound and video over the Internet, the greater the strain on the system. It can slow things down for everyone trying to use the system. I will talk more about bandwidth later.

Make sure you check with your teacher before going to music, sports, or video sites.

▶ Accidental Visits and Sites That Visit You

There are lots of adult-only Web sites on the Internet. I do not have to tell you that visiting them in or out of school is inappropriate. However, you may not have a choice. Sometimes you may click on a link that you think contains useful material, but end up at an adult site. What should you do then?

What you do depends upon how your school wants you to handle that kind of thing, but do not wait until it happens to think about the question. If you, your teacher, your class, or your parents have not discussed it, do it now! Some schools may want you to simply click off of the site and continue your work. Some may tell you to shut off the monitor and call a teacher.

If you accidentally come across an adult site, the images may be disturbing and something might happen that does not happen at other sites. What happens is something I call webnapping. The word is like kidnapping, but instead of stealing you, the site takes control of your Web browser and begins opening one window after another. If you close one, another opens up. You may not be able to get off of the site, even if you want to. You may have to shut down the computer to stop it.

It is very important that you discuss this with your teachers and parents. You should know what to do and you should be aware that you would not be in trouble if you accidentally come across a bad site and handle the situation correctly.

Chapter 4

Finding What You Want

Search engines are great tools. They help us locate information among the millions of pages out there on the Internet. However, if you are not an expert searcher, you usually end up with a lot of sites you do not need. There are also words that have more than one meaning. Conducting a search can bring up information you definitely have no use for.

Just because a site is brought up in a search engine, does not mean you have to click on it. Read the description of the site. Does it seem to have the information you want? If not, do not click on it. It can save you a lot of time and trouble.

If the description uses words you know are bad, do not click on the link. Be mature about it. The chances are that you have heard those words before. Do not make a big deal out of it. Just move on to useful information.

▶ WebChat, Instant Messaging, IRC, and Real-Time Communication

One of the most popular activities for children is live chat. Most schools only allow chat when a teacher is involved and part of the chat. As before,

Internet Addresses

You can avoid many of these problems by using kid-safe search tools. They do not have adult sites or other inappropriate material. Here are a few:

Yahooligans
<http://www.yahooligans.com>

KidsClick
<http://sunsite.berkeley.edu/KidsClick!/>

Ask Jeeves for Kids
<http://www.ajkids.com/>

Bartleby has dozens of research aids.
<http://www.bartleby.com/>

there are some very good reasons for this. They deal with privacy and safety. Using chat or instant messaging are fun activities, but they can also be dangerous ones.

Your parents have probably told you about talking to strangers. You know that you should never accept gifts, rides, or even talk to strangers. They can hurt you. Of course not all strangers will hurt you, but you have no way of knowing who will and who will not.

On the Internet, everyone you meet is a stranger, so it presents a problem. If you are in a chat room with your parent's permission, you are talking to strangers. You may talk to a person day after day. They may tell you all kinds of things about themselves. You may strike up a friendship, but THEY ARE STILL STRANGERS.

On Your Screen

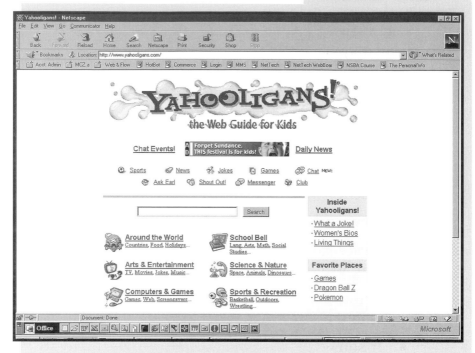

One of the best ways to make sure you get appropriate sites from your search engine is to use a kid-safe search tool like Yahooligans.

Everything they are telling you may be a lie. If they are the kind of people who want to harm you, they are not going to say, "Hi there. I'm a really bad person and I mean to do you harm." They will do everything they can to get you to trust them. They will flatter you and agree with you. You will think they're cool. Don't let them fool you. Don't share personal information with them. Don't agree to meet them without your parents and if they say anything or send you anything that you do not want or makes you feel uncomfortable, tell your parents or teachers immediately.

You never know whether the other person is who they say they are. That thirteen-year-old boy you are typing to might be who he says he is. However, it may be your ten-year-old sister playing a trick on you, or it may be a fifty-year-old man who means you harm.

Here are some very simple rules to follow when using chats:

- Always make sure you have your parent's or teacher's permission to use the chat.

- Never use your real name as your handle.

- Never share any personal information about you, your friends, or family.

- Remember that you have no way of knowing who the other person really is.

- If someone makes you feel uncomfortable, stop chatting with him or her and report the incident to an adult.

- Never call anyone on the phone that you met in a chat room, unless you have permission from your parents.

- Never meet anyone in person that you met in a chat room, unless you are with a parent.

Chapter 5

E-Mail Use and Abuse

E-mail is the most-used activity on the Internet. Schools have many different rules when it comes to e-mail. Some schools do not allow students to have e-mail accounts or to use their home e-mail accounts.

Here is a part of the section from our AUP:

> It is a violation of this AUP to send mail that is defamatory, abusive, obscene, profane, sexually oriented, threatening, racially offensive, or otherwise illegal. Anyone receiving such mail should refer it to the proper authorities for investigation.
>
> Southern Regional will provide e-mail accounts to all students who require them for curricular purposes. These accounts are for educational use only. Business, personal entertainment, or other non-educational use is to be avoided. Use of outside mail accounts or Web-based e-mail is prohibited. Accessing outside or Web-based accounts is a violation of this policy and will result in lost computer privileges.

If you understand that section, you see some rules are common sense. You should never do things through e-mail that you would not do in person or would not want others to do to you. Things like being rude or sending flames (angry messages) are things you would not do or want others to do to you.

Doing those sorts of things can be much worse when you do them on the Internet. If you write a note on paper in anger and say nasty things about someone, you may be sorry you said them later. Your words may do little or no damage, and if they do some harm, you might be able to smooth things over with an apology. However, if you sent a public message on the Internet in anger, it may reach hundreds or thousands of people. You can do serious damage to someone or you can make yourself look immature and thoughtless to all those people. You may not be able to correct that damage, or may end up having to apologize to hundreds or thousands of people.

Don't Be Angry:
An angry message is called a flame. It is considered rude and inappropriate to send one to someone.

The difference between note writing and the power of e-mail is a lot like learning about the power of cars compared to horses. Horse accidents can be damaging and hurt a few people, but car accidents can hurt a lot more people a lot more seriously. Written words of anger on paper can cause damage, but the same words in e-mail can cause much more damage.

▶ Spam

If your parents are not computer users and you talk to them about spam, they may think you are talking about a food made from ham scraps that was popular when they were growing up. You and I know that spam is junk mail that you get.

Spam comes in many forms. Every day I get messages telling me how I can get rich quick. I get messages to buy all kinds of things. I get messages about adult-only Web sites. I even get messages offering me college degrees without having to take classes. They are all examples of spam and are junk!

Some of them may sound tempting. They may sound like they really work. They may sound too good to be true. Well, trust me. They are too good to be true.

You may wonder why you are getting some of this garbage. Your parents may be angry about some of the mail you are getting and may think that you went to bad places you shouldn't go to, even though

Internet Addresses	Communication Facts	How Can I Be Safe?

You can find out more than you wanted to know about Spam and spam, by visiting these sites.

This is the official site of the Spam your parents will recognize.
<http://www.spam.com>

The Coalition Against Unsolicited Commercial E-mail is fighting spam through education and working to get laws passed.
<http://www.cauce.org>

Though there are no federal laws passed as I write this, there are state laws against spam. You can see if your state has such a law. Understanding them is something else. I suggest reading the summaries.
<http://www.spamlaws.com/state/index.html>

On Your Screen

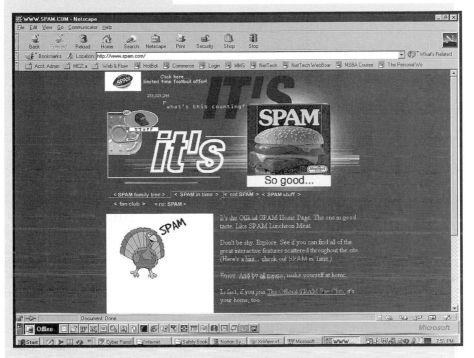

Internet users know the term spam to mean junk mail. When your parents hear the word, they may think of a type of food that was popular when they were kids. This is the Web site for the Spam your parents remember.

you did not go to any of those places. Why is this happening?

It is probably happening because you shared your e-mail address somewhere. Remember that COPPA was passed because Web sites were collecting information and selling it. If you share your information, it may get sold and resold. Unfortunately, there is no sure way to stop that material from coming in.

If you get spam, there is one thing you do not want to do. Do not follow the instructions to remove yourself from the list. If the message came from a spammer, instead of being removed from the list the only thing that will happen is that your reply confirms your address is active and real. That makes your address more valuable if they sell it.

If you follow the remove instructions, you might be removed, but you will probably just end up on more lists. When you get spam, do not waste your time responding to it. Just delete it!

▶ What Is Private and What Is Not?

When it comes to Internet e-mail, I can give you the answer to "What is private?" in two words— ALMOST NOTHING. I tell my students not to write anything they would not want to see printed in *The New York Times* the following day. When you send e-mail, it must pass through many computers on the way to its destination. The people in charge of those computers can read your mail. That does not normally happen, but it is possible.

The same is true for messages on your school network. Check your AUP to see if it says anything about monitoring e-mail. Here is what our AUP has to say.

> The system administrators will not intentionally inspect the contents of mail sent by one member to an identified addressee or disclose such contents to anyone other than the sender or an intended recipient without the consent of the sender or the intended recipient(s), unless required to do so by law or policies of the Southern Regional High School District or to investigate complaints regarding mail which may be in violation of this policy.

Okay, that is a mouthful. In plain English, it

says that we do not go snooping unless there is a reason. However, if there is a complaint about something, we will investigate and mail will be read.

E-mail monitoring is different from school to school and CIPA now requires schools to monitor student use of the Internet. Some schools might decide that reading e-mail is part of their monitoring policy.

Sometimes, just checking computer logs will trigger an investigation. Then, while investigating that AUP violation, others might be uncovered. For example, if someone on our system sends an inappropriate e-mail to someone else and a complaint

E-Mail Log

History: For all you Coke lovers...		
File Edit Message Conferencing Connection View Admin Help		
What	When	Who
✓ Created	12/15/00 4:20 PM	Art Wolinsky
✉ Sent	12/15/00 4:20 PM	Art Wolinsky
ᵒᵒ Read	12/15/00 4:24 PM	Art Wolinsky
ᵒᵒ Read	12/16/00 12:47 PM	BENSON CRAIG
▸✉ Forward	12/16/00 12:48 PM	BENSON CRAIG
ᵒᵒ Read	12/18/00 6:46 AM	MICHAEL SUSAN
ᵒᵒ Read	12/18/00 7:09 AM	GLENN BRUMMER
ᵒᵒ Read	12/18/00 7:18 AM	MARY DARNELL
ᵒᵒ Read	12/18/00 7:50 AM	LOUISE SUSAN
ᵒᵒ Read	12/18/00 7:57 AM	JEFFREY DEMARRAIS
ᵒᵒ Read	12/18/00 7:58 AM	ISABEL SOWLES

When an e-mail message is created, so is a message history like this one. It will show where the e-mail went and what those people did with it when they received it.

is made, an investigation is started. Our system allows us to track everything that happens to a message from the time it is created. If a person sent a message to twenty people, we can tell who received it and what they did with it.

Let us say that someone in school sent one of those messages forbidden by the AUP to twenty people in school. Would the twenty people who got the message be in trouble? The investigation would determine who gets in trouble and who does not. If you receive such a message, you should report it to your teacher, but unless the message is really bad, that may not happen. Though you could be in trouble for not reporting the violation, you probably will not be as long as you deleted the message right away. However, if you forward the message to someone else, that is the same as if you sent the message yourself, and you will most likely be in trouble.

If you ever get an e-mail that is disturbing or from someone you do not know, it is important to report it right away.

Sometimes you might get a message that is very disturbing and it may come from someone you do not know. In either case, it is very important that you report it. Though e-mail cannot hurt you, giving information that you should not give can hurt you.

If someone sends you material that upsets you through a school account, the school server will have records that will help track down the source of the problem much quicker than if the problem was on your home account. This is one important reason schools only want you to use a school e-mail account.

▶ You Cannot Hide!

Some people have found that they can send mail and put a fake return address on the message. They think that makes it impossible for people to know who they are. Because they think they cannot be traced, they may do something they are not supposed to do. That is a serious error on their part. The second you log on to any system, everything you do is recorded in log files.

We had a case where Student A sent a threatening message to someone and made it look like it was sent by Student B. Within one hour of getting the complaint, the message was traced back to Student A. That student was suspended and almost arrested.

| Internet Addresses | Communication Facts | How Can I Be Safe? |

If you want to get a more complete picture of hacking, what it is all about, and why it's not such a good activity to pursue, here are some sites to check out, and you do not even have to hack into them.

The Discovery Channel has a whole section devoted to the history of hacking.
<http://tlc.discovery.com/convergence/hackers/
    hackers.html>

USA Today has a large collection of articles about hackers in the news.
<http://www.usatoday.com/life/cyber/tech/cth313.htm>

The Theory Group is a security company that goes after hackers and protects companies.
<http://www.theorygroup.com/Theory>

Other students read about hackers and think it is cool, but it is illegal and very uncool. Even the most skilled hackers are very often caught and punished.

▶ Teachers Are Not the E-Mail Police

I do not want you to think that teachers or system administrators are sitting around watching everything you do. These examples represent the silly mistakes of a very small number of students. I only point them out to you because a small mistake can have a major impact on your life.

I tell students that if they ever consider doing something they know is wrong, to think about the worst possible outcome of their actions. Then assume that the worst would happen and decide if is worth doing something wrong.

The Internet is a valuable tool. Teachers do not want to take it away from you. They want to make it a safe, productive way for you to work and learn.

Chapter 6

Bandwidth and Hoses

Earlier, I mentioned that certain types of sites or Internet activities may be inappropriate because they use a lot of bandwidth. Your AUP may have sections that forbid game playing, recreational use of paint programs, viewing streaming video, or listening to music files without teacher permission. It is not because the school thinks these activities are a waste of time. It is because they can actually cost the school money and prevent others from doing schoolwork.

This is because these activities take a great amount of bandwidth. Bandwidth deals with the amount of information that flows through your Internet connection. Bandwidth costs money. You pay for bandwidth when you sign up for Internet at home, and your school pays for bandwidth when it buys its Internet connection.

Think of it like water flowing through a hose. The bigger the hose, the more water (information) it can carry. If you have a phone modem connection to the Internet, you are probably paying about twenty dollars a month. This is a small hose and you probably complain about having to wait for Web pages to load, especially if they contain video or music.

If you have a cable modem or other high-speed connection that gives you more bandwidth, you are probably paying about forty dollars a month. Web pages load much faster with a cable modem. You are paying more and you have more bandwidth.

It is possible to share one phone modem connection or one cable modem connection with more than one computer, but each computer you add will slow you down.

The bandwidth your school decides to buy depends on the number of computers that will be using the Internet. There are many different connections that schools can get. What they get is what they think is necessary to support learning. They

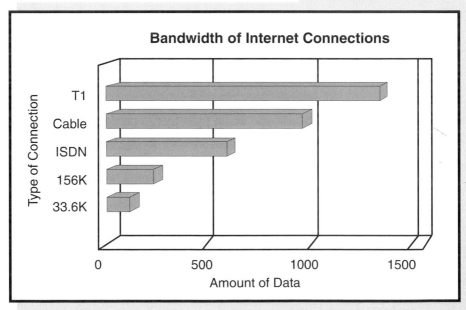

Bandwidth Chart

The type of Internet connection that is used greatly affects the amount of data that can be handled by the server.

Internet Addresses   Communication Facts   How Can I Be Safe?

If you want to see how fast your Internet connection is at home compared to school, you can go to one of these Web sites that will measure it for you.

MSN Computing Central

<http://computingcentral.msn.com/internet/speedtest.asp>

PC Pitstop

<http://www.pcpitstop.com>

The Internet Traffic Report monitors the flow of information through the major Internet service providers.

<http://www.Internettrafficreport.com/>

may have something called a T-1 line and may pay close to one thousand dollars a month.

Our two schools have almost two thousand computers. That is like splitting the one hose into two thousand hoses. Obviously, we need a big hose to feed that many connections. We have to pay a much higher price than you do at home. We calculate what we need by the kind of traffic we expect to have. If classes are visiting Web pages that contain text and graphics, the system works fine, because that is the kind of bandwidth it is prepared to handle. However, if some students are playing music, some are playing games, or some are viewing streaming video, this takes a great deal of bandwidth and things slow down.

All of a sudden, students who are viewing Web pages for class notice the pages are loading more slowly or stalling. This is because the students using video and games are hogging the bandwidth. They are preventing students from the learning that is supposed to be taking place in school. That is why those activities are inappropriate in school unless they are part of a lesson.

Remember that these sites are not bad sites. Visiting them at home may be perfectly acceptable, but in school they cause serious problems for others and are inappropriate use.

Chapter 7

Sharing or Piracy?

Most AUPs have a section that deals with software piracy. Software piracy is the copying of computer programs without paying for them. This is something that people often do outside of school. It is wrong anywhere, but if you do it through school computers you are in serious violation of the AUP.

Let us say that you just got a new computer game and your friend wants a copy. Do you let her borrow your disk or do you tell her to buy her own copy? If you give it to her, you are actually breaking a law known as the copyright law. It says the person who creates something owns it and is the only one who can give permission to distribute that material. Anyone else who wants to distribute it must have the permission of the author.

Someone put a lot of time and effort into creating the game. A company spent a lot of money to make copies, package it, and ship it to stores. The store paid people to stock the shelves and sell it. Every time someone makes a copy of that game and gives it to someone else, it is actually taking money away from the author, the store, and even the employees of the store.

When you give a program to a friend it is wrong. The chances are that if you get caught you will not be arrested, but you might get grounded or get a stern lecture. Even if you do not get caught, your conscience should bother you. On the other hand, if you are making copies and selling them, you can be in big trouble and could end up in court.

If you engage in any kind of piracy on school computers, it is serious. You are no longer breaking the law with your own computer. You are breaking the law with a computer that belongs to someone else. If the school allowed that to happen, they could be in big trouble with the community, the government, and the software company. Software piracy is no small matter.

▶ Copyright and Plagiarism

If you look on the page before the table of contents in this book, you will see a copyright notice. It says, Copyright © 2003 by Art Wolinsky. That means I wrote this book and own the rights to it. No one can make copies of it without my permission. It would not be right for someone to make copies of the book and give it to their friends. That would be like stealing money from me. (You don't want to do that. I'm a nice guy and never hurt you.) It is a lot like software piracy. In both cases, you are stealing something that does not belong to you.

But, wait a minute. If you are familiar with making Web pages, you know that people take things from Web sites without permission. Is there really anything wrong with that? The answer is yes. You should never take things that do not belong to you without permission. It does not matter whether

they are objects or thoughts. If they belong to someone else, you should get permission to use them.

Now, there are no copyright police that will
arrest you if you were to make a copy of this book
for yourself, if you were to copy a chapter and send
it to a friend, or if you took a picture or information from a Web site. However, doing that can get
you in big trouble in school if you were to copy parts
of a document and hand it in to your teacher without giving credit to the author.

This is a special kind of copyright violation that
is called plagiarism. Plagiarism takes place when
you copy someone else's work and hand it in as
your own. If you plagiarize in elementary school,
your teacher will probably correct you. If you plagiarize in high school, you may fail the assignment.
If you plagiarize in college, you might fail the course
or even get expelled from school. In education,

Internet Addresses | Communication Facts | How Can I Be Safe?

**The Oregon State Library has some great tools.
Depending on your age, visit their Elementary or
Secondary pages.**
<http://www.oslis.k12.or.us>

**Regardless of your age, be sure to visit their tool for
creating citations. You fill in the blanks and it
creates the proper format that you can copy and
paste into your paper.**
<http://www.oslis.k12.or.us/elem/howto/citeintro.html>

Midlink Magazine **for Kids has a good set of
resources for copyright and citations.**
<http://www2.ncsu.edu/ncsu/cep/ligon/citing.html>

stealing other people's thoughts and words is a serious thing.

That does not mean you cannot use material from this book or other books. You can use portions of anyone's work in small chunks, as long as you give proper credit to the author. Giving credit is called citing the material. There are special ways that you make citations.

▶ Housekeeping

Is your mom or dad always telling you to keep your room neat and uncluttered? Well, in school, your system administrator may be telling you the same thing about your disk storage area. Here is what our AUP says about electronic housekeeping.

> The system administrators reserve the right to set quotas for disk usage on the system. A member who exceeds his quota will be advised to delete files to return to compliance. A member who remains in noncompliance of disk space quotas after seven (7) days of notification will have their files removed by a system administrator.

The English translation is that you have a limited amount of storage area on the school's network. If you go over that storage limit, the system administrator will send you a message to clean up your storage area. If you do not do it within seven days, he can remove all of your files.

Suppose you are working on a big project and you need all of your space and more. Should you worry? Does that mean you will not be able to do the project? I do not think so. The AUP is there as a guide and it is designed to help you. Disk quotas are set to prevent people from letting junk files clog up the system and take up valuable space. If you are working on a project and need extra space, you should just write an e-mail to the system administrator explaining the situation and asking for additional space. It is also a good idea to send a copy of the message to your teacher. I bet you will have the extra space you need and perhaps a nice note thanking you for your polite request.

As long as we are on the topic of space, it looks like I am running out of it. I hope you now understand that the reason behind AUPs and many rules is to keep you safe, protect your privacy, and make your education more enjoyable and productive. If you do, then Web and I have done our jobs and are happy.

Your teachers and your parents know that the Internet is a very powerful and useful tool. They want you to be able to use it safely and productively so that you can carry on the job of making the world a better place.

The more you understand, the better off you will be, and the better off your children will be when you grow up and are in charge of setting guidelines and rules for them.

See you around cyberspace.

See You Later . . .
Well, it's been fun, and we sure learned a lot about rules and safety of surfing the Web. I can't wait to do some Internet surfing! See you soon!

Glossary

Acceptable Use Policy (AUP)—Guidelines that schools and libraries create so that their users understand how to use their computer network safely and efficiently.

bandwidth—The measure of the speed of your Internet connection is the bandwidth. The greater the speed, the greater the bandwidth.

cable modem—Special modem that works with a high speed Internet connection supplied by a cable company.

Children's Internet Protection Act (CIPA)—A law that requires schools to install technology, usually filters, to protect children from harmful images online, and to create online safety programs.

Children's Online Privacy and Protection Act (COPPA)—A law that protects the privacy of children online. It requires Web-site owners to get parental permission before allowing visits or collecting any information from children under the age of thirteen.

commercial Web site—A Web site that is created by a business that sells a product or service.

copyright law—Law that protects the authors of any kind of writing.

CyberAngels—The largest volunteer online Internet safety organization in the world.

filters—Computer software that prevents Internet users from getting to Web sites that contain material that may be considered harmful to children.

flames—Angry messages.

hacking—Though hacking can mean many things, it usually involves breaking into computers.

information revolution—There have been a number of information revolutions. The first took place when the printing press was invented and ordinary people could own books. The latest information revolution is due to the Internet. It gives people the ability to get more information than ever and to share information like never before.

netiquette—These are unwritten rules about how people should communicate and behave online. It is one part of netizenship.

netizenship—All the ways a person behaves online. It is much like citizenship, the way a person behaves in the face-to-face world.

Oregon Trail—From about 1835 to 1869, the Oregon Trail was the only overland route to the West Coast of the United States. Half a million people traveled over the trail in wagon trains, on horses, and on foot.

plagiarism—Using the work of others without giving them credit, or presenting it as your own words.

quota—The amount allowed. This often refers to disk space quotas, the amount of space you have for storing things on a network.

software piracy—Making illegal copies of computer software to give to others.

spam—Electronic junk mail that you did not request and most likely do not want.

spammer—A person or company that sends spam.

system administrator—The person in charge of a computer network.

T-1 line—A high speed Internet connection used by schools and businesses.

telecommunications—Any kind of electronic communication.

transportation revolution—In the 1800s, horses began to be replaced by trains, cars, and other mechanical means of transportation. This change was called the transportation revolution.

webnapping—When you visit a site that does not allow you to leave and keeps popping up another window every time you try to leave the page.

Further Reading

Gralla, Preston. *Online Kids: A Young Surfer's Guide to Cyberspace*. New York: John Wiley and Sons, 1999.

Pedersen, Ted. *How to Find Almost Anything on the Internet: A Kid's Guide to Safe Searching*. New York: Penguin Putnam Books, 2000.

Rothman, Kevin F. *Coping with Dangers on the Internet: A Teen's Guide to Staying Safe Online*. New York: The Rosen Publishing Group, Inc., 2000.

Whitcombe, Dan. *Dk.com Kid's Guide to the Internet*. Dorling Kindersley Publishing, Inc., 2001.

Index